Dan Corjescu

**Kisses from the Apocalypse
(And Other Small Things)**

Dan Corjescu

KISSES FROM THE APOCALYPSE (AND OTHER SMALL THINGS)

Bibliografische Information der Deutschen Nationalbibliothek

Die Deutsche Nationalbibliothek verzeichnet diese Publikation in der Deutschen Nationalbibliografie; detaillierte bibliografische Daten sind im Internet über http://dnb.d-nb.de abrufbar.

Bibliographic information published by the Deutsche Nationalbibliothek

Die Deutsche Nationalbibliothek lists this publication in the Deutsche Nationalbibliografie; detailed bibliographic data are available in the Internet at http://dnb.d-nb.de.

Cover image: Art by Cameron Gray www.ParableVisions.com
The Heart (Cover)
Eternal Kiss
Was
Out of My Skin
Eyes

ISBN-13: 978-3-8382-1123-7
© *ibidem*-Verlag, Stuttgart 2022
Alle Rechte vorbehalten

Das Werk einschließlich aller seiner Teile ist urheberrechtlich geschützt. Jede Verwertung außerhalb der engen Grenzen des Urheberrechtsgesetzes ist ohne Zustimmung des Verlages unzulässig und strafbar. Dies gilt insbesondere für Vervielfältigungen, Übersetzungen, Mikroverfilmungen und elektronische Speicherformen sowie die Einspeicherung und Verarbeitung in elektronischen Systemen.

All rights reserved. No part of this publication may be reproduced, stored in or introduced into a retrieval system, or transmitted, in any form, or by any means (electronical, mechanical, photocopying, recording or otherwise) without the prior written permission of the publisher. Any person who does any unauthorized act in relation to this publication may be liable to criminal prosecution and civil claims for damages.

Printed in the EU

La raíz de todas las pasiones es el amor. De él nace la tristeza, el gozo, la alegría y la desesperación.

Lope de Vega

Si nada nos salva de la muerte, al menos que el amor nos salve de la vida.

Pablo Neruda

Contents

Part I Kisses from the Apocalypse 9

Part II Earlier Poems 97

Part III Environmental Ethics.. 107

Part IV Medea in Hell 115

Part V Final Kiss 125

Part I
Kisses from the Apocalypse

Part 1
Kisses from the Apocalypse

Pity

I feel very sorry for those
Who are able to read
My poetry right

For they are in hell

And every word
Will fall on them

Like a boulder

Like a curse

The Owls of Minerva

This life
Was a set up

To be fire

To be flood

To be warning

And at the very end

Crazy dark owls

Burst out of my chest

Laughing

Two Hearts

The cunt
Cut my heart
In two

It was a clean cut

Not much blood

Anyway

Now I've got two hearts

One that feeds

And

One that starves

The blood

Craft Crazy

I try to leave the
Similes and Metaphors
Behind me
Like dark senseless animals

I'm a butcher
And my poetry is meat

I hack at it

Like life at me

I shred my lines like dirty snow

I gnaw dead sonnets

I growl at my images

I put my face in a bowl

And mash it up with bloodied rhyme

I look for the cleaver that gleams

And stretch out my neck

Like a finger that bleeds

Liberty

The Statue of Liberty

Is a crazy old slut

Promising you the greatest
Fuck

If you'd only feed your guts
Into her green torch
Of trumped up Liberty

If you'd only give her
Your mind
Burnt on the speed
Of Atomic Promises

If you'd only disembark
Into her deep cunt
Of filthy money

"C'mon you poor bastard!"
She says
"Shut up and kneel--the gods are waiting"

Fuck You

My favorite poem is called:

"Fuck You"

I like to start my day with it

And end my nights with it

I like to recite it

To all those

Waiting to eat me

Waiting to fuck me

With their very own

Special poetry

Blood Red Moon

There's a blood red moon tonight
Blood red
Blood red
Blood red
Like the blood in my veins
I stare
helplessly
At the celestial blood spot
And think:

Circulation

Don't Force It

Don't force it

Turning plants to steam
Rivers into hydraulic forces
The wind into horses

Don't force it

Knowledge
Is the burnt Face of the World

By your side

That I cannot be by your side
While the world dies
Is a gratuitous affliction

That I cannot caress you
While the winds subside
And the ocean swells retire
Is a blue pulse of painful resignation

That we cannot make love
While the stars occult
And the Earth hides
Before the final order of execution

That All is Death girding
My lush sentiment
For Eros born too late
In the Winter of Desperate Excuses

And suddenly

Your hair catches fire
Your eyes burst into flame
Your body is a furnace

The glowering heat of this Last Love
Is my Testament to All that Might Have Been

Perfect

Perfect are you to me
In my willful stubbornness
Against all imperfection

I will not see
The cage that you offer me
The blood pact
That holds me

I knowingly love in crime
And my passion is sacrilege

But as we all fall down
And are vanquished

My trembling hands fashion
A Weak Altar

From which I drink my own body's wine
Ever hoping for the copious blood
Of The World
To quench this burning thirst
For the Divine

Madman

I am a madman
searching for God

I search for him in my sleep
I search for him in the junkyards
I search for him when I'm drunk
I search for him amidst the cries of the weak
I search for him in missile silos
I search for him in the lost eyes of Junkies
I search for him in Nuclear Power Plants
I search for him when I make love (especially then)
I search for him in the strange silence of plants

I search for him when the sea is angry
I search for him in the cruelest betrayal
I search for him in the graveyards

I search for him

For I am a madman
Oblivious to history
Deaf to Philosophy
Blind to Religion

I see worlds rising

I will meet him at the other side of the last dawn

Morning Poems

I'm up in the morning
reading poems

The sunlight bends in my hands

I see birds
who remind me of irrepressible lightness

I am forgetful
for a moment
of who I am
and I am thankful
for this

I am reading
poems in the morning

And I feel
just for a moment
the furthest arc of bliss

Out of my skin

How can I walk out of my skin
gently?

Walk deeply down ephemeral
paths

Find questions that

release me

Will anyone give me a hand?

I think not

For we are imminently

singular

Born to whimper

alone

All else is the illusion
of unity

I can only transcend
my own eyes

I'd like to borrow God's
of course

But I can't

But right now

I'm busy making myself
porous

slowly emptying out into the universe

seeking the improbable
holiness
of disembodied grace

Time weaves

Time weaves

and we are
condemned
to pick
out
And live
all the strands
from
blood red
to
darkest black

Eyes

We have betrayed
the eyes of children

A vast skein
of lies betrayals murders
is the real playground of their vision

Better to have been born
blind
to a world so achingly
ugly

But

However

We wait

For at least one child
to raise a fistful
of hot sand
to sear
the world

to cauterize
its agony

to bring the Argus-storm
of new Being

Great River

I should not think about you
If you were not
The Great River of Being

In your sunlight
I will not

I wish not
To stoop
In your Gardens
To taste your false delights

You are Presence

You are beyond denial

Yet I am a small
Curmudgeonly Being

And I will bite
All of Existence

Just to provoke
The slightest cringe
Of Otherness
Of Self-revealing light

Poetry Refuge

Oh! Do not seek refuge in poetry!
This mad swirl of mind!
Do not launch off the greenest of waterfalls
And ride the peaks of Boreal Winds!
Do not eat of the fruit of the Elysian fields
And speak with the smiling sly Socrates!
Beware a fleet of Portuguese Galleons!
Beware the bound feet of a Chinese maid!
All and Nothing is this magic fragile isle
All and Nothing will be made and unmade!
Leave the Mandrake root!
Leave the shared Witch's Eye!
Make haste through this Kingdom of Hurling Sound!
Reach breathless the Shores of The Real
Look not back at the Phantoms in the Forest
Leave behind the eternal fires that inspire
Renounce thy Crown and Kingship in Poetry!
And now once done:
Breathe

Was

"Was" is a sad little word
Like a slab of concrete

Nothing moves in "Was"
Even steel is more flexible

"Was" is a fossil

Of love of hate of desire of pain

"Was" is forever cut off from us
Even though it continuously hits us
On the head

All of us are destined to live
In the Kingdom of Was

Forever

The only questions are:

In what perpetual pose
In what defiant act of eternal disdain

Encounter

Bukowski meets Plotinus
Now that would be some kind of Poet!

Bukowski

Bukowski

He was an Early Angel of the Apocalypse

Meat and Shit

Cigarettes and Sex

He gave no apologies

He was hard and fulminous
In his love

He left the light on in the bathroom
So that *We* don't forget to flush

He's fucking Angels now
While God tries to adjust his Angles

Hosanna!

No Luck

I just have no luck

To be stuck
in a world
that's a video game
called "Marx and Engels Drunk"

I just have no luck

To be a poet stuck
in quicksand

To slowly drown
while gulping down the brown shit of civilization

To be stuck
inside Fascist Cunts
that sell Love on Cable

To be stuck inside a jam
inside a fuck up inside
a sham

The Laws of Physics say:

Go Fuck Yourself You Schmuck! You have no luck

Funny thing

A funny thing happened on the way to Existence.

I bargained with the Angels for a half price on
Materiality

I pushed to play cards with God before the onset of Eternity
(Ever hoping for a straight flush)

I interminably philosophized with Lucifer
(Eventually driving him nuts... Yes, I'm responsible for
the Celestial Revolution)

I tried to organize a citizen's fire-brigade for the Stars of the Empyrean

I wondered aloud if sex was the best possible algorithm

In short, I was a cosmic nuisance

And finally for all my trouble making

I was made Adam

Dumb as all fuck

And then pulling from me
(While I slept no less!)
A treacherous cunt
Called Eve

And then

Tossed out of Paradise
On a technicality!

All this shit
finally got to me

And I went down on my knees
and wept
And from that
came the first flowers

Fucked

When I fuck you
I fuck a ton of gangsters

All ready
to cut my dick off

Switchblade Love
Is most fun

Bullets and Blood
Deep Fuck Label

And yet

I can't get you out of my head

A thousand Oceans press on me

This, man, is the Deepest Fuck
Where there's nowhere to go
And no way to cum

COVID

Persona
Is
A mask

A
Person
Is
A
Mask

It's
Mask
All
The
Way
Down

COVID
Just
Outed you

Life's
Funny
That
Way

UFO

My neighbor
Told me
He saw a UFO

I think

My neighbor
Is stranger
Than
That

He watches the skies

He believes them
To be inhabited

By superior beings

All I see
Is a screaming silence

My neighbor
Is happier
Than me

Scar

I run my fingers
Over my scar

It is more than me

It is deep

If you look
Closely enough
You can see
A face

Mocking

A life

Cities

I hate you my cities!

For you have made me

Sao Paulo of my
Hot wet birth

New York
Of the sacred
curses

Prague
O Prague!
You were
The most beautiful!

Sofia
At the end
Of my earth

Ulm
Where I learned
To ride my bike
Again

And now
Plittersdorf

Not a city

But a village

Where I see
The fantastic tops
Of my cities

Calling to me distant

Calling back that which they own

Running out of Fucks

There's not much
Time left

I know it

You know it

There's not much
Time left

For me to meet you

For me to fuck you

For me to forget you

But I never forget
A momentous fuck

Ever

I count up
All the fucks
Of my life

Just to eke out
One lousy prayer

Pump

How many Cunts
Do I have to
Pump

To get me outta here

To remove my innerness

To show me a way

To open
Exhaustedly

To where
No Sea Creatures
Can
Emerge

Old Cat

There's an old cat
Watching me

It's eyes
Crusty
With hate

It's tongue
A little
Pink snake

There's an old cat
Watching me

It would kill
Me if it could

It's a nasty animal

Humming
Purring

With hate

It dares me
To cross it

So to show
It's final claws
Of Fate

Fever

The Fever has broke

Like old bones

Industrial waste

Has made haste

And my face

Is all oil and dust

There is no place for you here

You are not welcome

During this last evening

I want to pass
My hands
Through my heart
Alone

I want to break my fingers

One by one

Slow

It does not matter

I am a smoldering wreck

A uranium pile of
Forgetfulness

You do not owe me
Anything

No one owes
Me
Anything

The wind fits
Tight
On me

The Fever has broke

And I am
Hard as diamond

Standing on the rim

Of an angry
New
Volcano

Shock

I turned a street corner
And found Love
Shot dead

It was a clean shot
To the head

Fingers spread

Legs apart

A shocked sudden
Look

I didn't know what
I was going to tell
The police

Or the medics

Upon their eventual
Arrival

I just stared at the
High Hot Orange Sun

And wept

Music

Stab me with
Your song

Let each
Note
Destroy
Me

The
Annihilation
Of
Music

I love
The sound
Of
My perfect death

Caesar Speaks Again

I hated, I loved, I lived.

If I Should Think Of Love

If I should think of love

Stuff my mouth
Full of dirty old rags

If I should think of love

Set the hounds
Upon my liver

Hang my heart
Upon a meat hook

Give me all the wrong
Directions
To the Isle

Deny me drink, food, and
Books

Let me walk naked
Through the moon's
Cold white fire

Drown me in
Cheap wet excuses

Let me not hear, see,
Or speak

If I should think of love
Again

Burn all my poetry

Bad Habits

Sometimes
I think
To be
A great poet

You have to be

A drunk
A drug addict

A womanizer
At least

Sadly

I'm none of these

I'm worse

I'm a God eater

Bridge

I see a dark bridge
Before me

I dare not cross it

It is dark
In the day

It is darker
At night

My fear of it
Is the ichor
Of my life

I see a dark bridge
Before me

And I must cross it

It will have me
Transit

It will push me across

It will drown my panic
With each footfall

The bridge is getting
Darker
As I approach it

As I put all
The light of the world
Into my freezing pockets

I am there now

In the dark

And there is no end in sight

Upon this bridge
That I must cross

And a dreadful thought
Passes

There may yet
Be another

Even more terrible

Sex Ban

Let sex
Be not your master

Let sex
Beg at the door

Let it
Writhe
And

Seethe
As a blue storm

Let sex
Be not your master

Let it die
A while

For you to relearn
The strength
Of other things

To reteach
The hidden things

Stop worshiping
Cunts and Whores

Go outside a while

Take off your burning skin

Fill your mouth with
Beautiful words

Now go

And

Fuck

The world

With

An

Open

Heart

Waiting

You
Betrayed me
Before
I even
Knew
You

Your beauty
Could never
Pay the rent

Nor did I want you too

Drunk on passion
I wanted to make you
My story

I wanted you to fill
The pages
Of a thousand books

Your beauty

Tastes better

Than your betrayal

Stinks

I look over my shoulder

Hoping for a glimpse

I turn the door knob

Hoping

I pace the floors

Slack-jawed and dreamy

I move my body

Carefully

In incantation

You are the Rite
Of the Fool

And I know

No greater

Pleasantness

Than

This

One

A school of fish
Swims to me

Birds
Crane their
Necks
Towards me

Dogs
Strain in my
Direction

Is it just me?

Or does it seem

That we all

Want

to be

One

Again?

Dreams

Some Men
Dream
Of a life
Among the stars

Other Men
Dream
Of a sandwich

And still
Many more
Dream
Of a fresh young
Cunt

Dreams

You
Can't
Count
Them

There are too many

And never enough

School

In school
I had to
Sit
In a chair
All day

That was boring

Luckily
There where girls
To dream at

At University
We sat too
And talked
About philosophy

That was better

And there, too, were girls

I have forgotten all that I have learned now

But not the girls

Expert

I don't want to be
An expert
In anything

To be expert
Means you
Have died
A little bit
To the world

But don't worry

We all know
I'm a fool

Wrapped up
In Believing
Like a rose-bud
In June

Rain

I'm ambivalent
About
The rain

Is it
A slow-handed
Assassin

Killing rocks
And
Leveling
Mountains

Or is it
Gold
As Bukowski
Says

A bit of both
It seems

It can break stone

It can lift flowers
Out of their earthen
Beds

It can carry away villages

It can delight
Fishes

It can wake
Hollow men

It can break
Trees
As well
As kiss
Them

It can tear up asphalt
Or cool the day down
For children to play

It can do all these things

And more

Rain

I'm beginning to like you

Truest Whores

Whores
Are
Honest
People

I give you
Something
You give
Me
Something

No bullshit
No flowers
No promises

I give you
Something

Whores
Are the truest expression of Man

As He is

Not as He
Imagines
Himself

To be

Girls

I have pretty prison
Guards

I'm their favorite pet

I'm held in chains
Of sex and of regret

Which I fashioned
For myself

I stare into their
Eyelashed abysses

Every day I
Ejaculate
Ablution

Every day
I seek the formula
For my chemical
Solution

There isn't any

It's hopeless

The Eternal Feminine
Is the High Vault
Of my particular
Damnation

My perfumed
Straitjacket
Of Eternity

Stop

I want to live
But I can't

I want to love
But I can't

I want to dream
But I can't

Life is an extortionist

At the beginning of this street
I was mugged

I was knifed
Deep
In the gut

They came out
To get me

To rob me of
My bones

To carve me up
On a capitalist table

To make my mind
Rhyme with stone

A STOP sign
Is my mark
Of Cain

They're conceiving
Of accidents
From the mild
To the fatal

Without any legs
I'll get to No-where
Fast

Limping across
The Arc of Existence

Waiting for some Noah
To take me
To a new world
At the last

Final Days

I'm counting down
To my own death

To the sound
Of lousy Cunts

Squealing
Deliriously
Over my pain

To kids laughing in my face

To policemen with big hands

To a universe that doesn't
Give a damn

I'm counting down
To my own death

Day by Day
Minute by Minute

I won't be able to steal
A second
From what is written

Bukowski's optimism
Was pretty
But it was innocent

I am a firefly of fate
I flicker for a moment

And am gone

A small very small
Intense light of pain

I am counting down
To my own death

Will you count with me?

Condemned

To the prisoners
That sit
Waiting for death

Know
That it is not your
Fault

You were fashioned
For this

To kill to maim
To rebel

The universe made you
To this

And no other

To be hated by the others
To be condemned
To be killed

To kill yourself
In pain
In remorse

You have done
Horrible things

That we want

To quickly put away

To shock the ugliness
Of Existence
Into oblivion

To numb the veins
Of our irremediable
Failures

To put to death
Our knowledge

Of things as they are

Of the Rule of Imperfection

Of the murderer
Waiting for any chance
In you

Great

To walk among the great poets
Is to live again

To reengineer
Your own birth

My ears become
Astronomical
Radio Dishes
For signals
Of the divine

Each word a new liquor

Each rhyme a release
From the falsities of life

Each metaphor
A transit point
To an alternate me

In a better universe

Each idea a new fountain of life

I am perpetually drunk
On great poetry

It is only in drowning
That I breathe

94

94
Is the number
Of my house

It is also
The number of death
Of a great poet

I didn't know it
At first

But we are brothers
Born of a distant light

Raging existentialists

One a drug addict
An alcoholic

The other an impossible
Abstinent

No matter

We both drink the ambrosia
Of the flesh

We see the intense light
Between
Women's legs

We feel the inner seam

Of the collective destiny

We like to miss trains

We like to mock power

We find in the smallest things
The biggest Redemption

And we walk with the Gods

Ruminating

Over

94 ways to live

And

94 ways to die

C.B.

A Charles Bukowski
Poem

Makes me
Breathe
New Air

See New Light

It makes me
Want to promise
Myself to myself

And write
And write
And write

Weather Report

I check the weather
Report
Like a religion

I want to know
What's coming

Where and when

What, in part, will happen to me

Today Tomorrow even Yesterday

I check the weather report
Like an ancient priest
His entrails

I search for signs

Of better days

And curse
Premeditatively
The worse

I want to know
The future

To control it

To bend the rain and the sun
And the storm

To the rhythms of
My automatically wringing hands

To my willfully lost imagination

I check the weather report

Because I am cloudy
Because I am wet
Because I am drenched

With Doubt

Because I fear death

I check the weather report

Mystery

My love is a mystery

It catches flies
Like spiders

It hangs
Like old paint

It refuses
Like cats
Refuse

It's a tired
City street

My love is a mystery

Where I sit
And eat

All by myself

Phrase

To say "I love you"
Is so bourgeois

Does it mean
I own you?

For you
To take your place
On the factory floor
Of love

Or behind a desk
Stamping endless papers

Of my communiques of love

"I love you"
Comes like a bullet
Like a serial killer

Give me your time
Give me your bread

Lay yourself on the bed
Like a crimson ribbon

Open your legs
For a parade of flags
A sex-army
Born to conquer

Next time
Instead
Of
"I love you"

I'll say

Nothing

And gently

Wash your hands

Death wish

Sometimes
I wish
you'd kill me

Just
One time

To die
And
Forget
The Living-Dying

To be oblivion

To be uninteresting
To dogs
And women

To leave loose change
Forever on the floor

To be insensate
To gardens

To be a sack of death
Everybody forgets

To leave emotions

To leave

And thereby

Return

Entrance

The softness
Of your
Entrance

Explodes
Like
A bomb
In
Me

And I
Spend
All night
Picking
Out
The Pink Red
Shrapnel

Caressing
Each
And
Every
Deadly
Piece

I want to
Rerun
Your
Steps

Although
I'm tired
Of
Hunting
The moon

I will
Sit

Fast
In Time

Fabulously
Broken
By
You

Bukowski

Bukowski!

You are a poet of
Fate

Admirer

Your beauty
Is the best
Apology
For Death

It is a symmetry
Fashioned
By Angel Breath

It is a reflection
Of the Core
Of Everything

My eyes
Are jealous
Of what
They
See

And I think:

God may indeed be beautiful

Name

To say your name
Is to speak
The Infinite

To round
My mouth
Over Gigantic
Forests

To let
My tongue
Slide
Down
The Waterfall
Of Being

To feel
My teeth
Rattle
With the
Coming
Of your
Seasons

Exhale

Inhale

I say your name

As a magical
Ladder
To God

Sisyphus

I keep running in place
In front of impossibly
High mountains

The Gods gave me
No stone
To roll

Just to run in place

Panting
Like a dog

Not to move an inch

To remain in place

To remember
That only Gods can
Truly move

While the cursed
Revolve around
Themselves
Eternally

Place

This is the place
Where all Mothers
Burn

This is the place
Where birth
Is a curse

This is the place
Where Death
Gets fully reimbursed

People have
Numbers
On their arms
Without knowing

People are
Herded
Into shops
Into sex
Into murder

People
Never
Wake
Up

They're born to sleep

They're born to eat

They're born to leave shit

And they're born to make
Ever bigger
Cages

For ever greater
Fools

Goethe

"Das ewige Weibliche zieht uns hinan"

It's true
For me

Beyond dead worlds
Beyond horrid deeds

I set a thousand Beatrices

High

Higher

Highest

Within
My inner
Aurelian
Sky

Missing you

I miss you
Who never
Had you

The broken
Earth
Of my heart

I want to give you
Sea water

I want to give you
Flasks of dirt

I want to give you
The secret of trees

I want to branch
Into you

You

Who are the
Pith
Of Awe

Tiresias

If you know
The truth
You will
Deny it
And call
Me mad

If you do not know
The truth
You, too,
Will call me
Mad

Like Tiresias
I walk the earth
Rhyming in Riddles
Raising a Song

From the bowels
Of the Earth

Silence

This silence
Has been imposed
Upon me

Like and unlike
Prometheus
I am chained
To an uncaring cliff

Mouth bolted
Shut

The sea cannot
Touch me

The sky cannot
Heal me

The earth cannot
Nourish me

I am an outcast
In this life

Silent
Within
Silence

In my breast

A snake

The struggling
Sound

Kills me

Kisses

Kisses from the Apocalypse
I send you

These perfect, last things

Where love
Is heated statues

And Polar Bears
Digital Enchantments

Where people
Are last on the Menu

And Rocket Ships
In Vast Deserts
Stand Sentinel
Waiting for the
Messiah

I kiss you
To taste you
To see
If I want
To eat you

Blood
Sweat
And
Saliva
Are at
A premium

Where lovers
Pour
Gasoline
On
Themselves

And burn
Like falling stars
In the acid rain

New King

When Cockroaches
Will be Kings

They will
Scamper
Up and down
Giant
Left-over

Things

In and Out
Of dolls'
Mouths

Atop
Ghostly rafts
Of refrigerators

Squiggling
Between
Lines
Of radioactive
Newspaper

They will be legion
They will be a giant mass
Of black things

Their antennas
Outstretched
In a quizzical manner

Over a Vast Empire
Of Dead Ape Shit

Bath

I was taking
An acid bath
Just the other
Day

Trying to remove
Everything
About me

To get past
The bone
Of things

I
Finally
Got
Down
To
Nothing

And
Then
Beyond

Nothing

A child's
Broken
Hand

Flame

I like to be with you
Even though you want
To bury me

I like to sit next to you
Even though you want
To steal my soul

I want to kiss you
Even though
You want to poison me

You're my little love-hate
My puzzle of the world

I like to play
With all your pieces

Because I know

It pisses you off

Each jigsaw key

Brings a little more freedom

Brings a little more pain

While I stubbornly love you

Trying to work out

The gas stove

The flame

Celluloid Cowboy

I rode a dead horse
into a ghost town

Everyone was dead
So I didn't have to
Talk much

In my loneliness
I broke into a song
That went something like this:

I've seen highs
And I've seen lows

But nothing like this

I loved you one hot June
Even though
I knew
You were of the Demon

We played in the waters
We played in the sands

And I swore that the Sun
On that Day
Was but your tiny accompaniment

But to love a witch
Properly

You have to be a Devil

An Angel in Hell
Is a comic figure

And an Angel in Love

Well
That never happens

Except in movies

Two Poets

Charles Bukowski
Charles Baudelaire

You nasty
Beautiful
Creatures

You dine
On the
Carcass
Of men

You spit
On the
Night

You rape
Existence
As it has
Raped
You

You quietly
Weep
Filling
The gutters

You enter

Whores
Like
Cathedrals

You two men
Of spleen
Of fire
Of refusal

You offer
Posterity
Sublime
Cigarettes
And
The
Ecstasy
Of
Opium

And I accept

I accept
The rough mountainous
Shoulders
Of high
Poetry

Where I lay my head

And write

Immortal Poet

Bukowski

Wrote
Immortal
Poems

With
His
Pants
Down

While
Taking
A
Shit

After
Vomiting

After
Restless
Fucking
(Working he called it)

He just
Dumped
Blood
On the
Typewriter

He
Uncorked
His mind
Into
Cheap
Beer
Glasses

He drowned

His guts
On paper

He was
Los Angeles'
Sad Dionysius

But the gods (in whom he believed)
Kept him

Kept him
Close

To better hear
His groaning
Midnight Messages
To Olympus

To The Twenty-Second Century

To you
Who won't
Read me
In
The twenty second
Century

Salve!

I hope
You're not
Fully
Lobotomized
Commercialized
Commodified

I hope
You can
Still think

You may

Not have
Sinks

You may
Not have
Toilets

You might
Not even
Have to
Take a
Shit

But will you
Still need to love?

To read and write
Poetry?

On these questions
Depend

Whether the

Human experiment

Was
An open ended

Or

Prematurely told

Joke

Soldier

You shower me in war

You tighten the bow

Your arguments
Are destiny

Cacaphony
Envelopes me

The madness
Enters my veins

I am drunk on Ares

I'll rip your lungs out

I'm your ever green soldier

Ready for a smoke, a bullet, a death

Give me my marching orders

My broken love
Is your grenade

Greatest

My greatest wish
Is to weave
Forever into you

To have
The Seasons
Of life
Wave through you

To make you
An astronomical map
Of the most beautiful longing

I want future men and women

To breathe through you

I want the blinding Green
Of existence
To vertically explode
In you

I want atoms to dance

To speak you

But alas

I am a bad poet

But even the worst poets

Hope

Birdie

This little bird
fights his day

Leans hard
Into flight

Darts his eyes
In search of
rare earth

Displacing space
creating new time

A pioneer of the every day

A hungry arrow lifted
by hopeful wings

This little bird
magnificent

A Simple Question

How many poets have
to die

Before

The world
>   really
>   loves

A flower?

What's the Use?

I'm not sure
How powerful
God is

He can't pay my
Electric bill

He can't teach me
How to swim

He can't make me
A martini

So what Good is He?

Well

Sometimes

He allows me to see
The diaphanous Wings of Being

A Little Prayer

I have never abandoned you
My Lord

Although I have always walked
Alone

I have never abandoned you
My Lord

Although I have suffocated
In Forests of Fire

I have never abandoned you
My Lord

Although I have carried my hope
Like a dead stag upon my shoulders

I have never abandoned you
My Lord

Although arrows of malice and of hate
Have pierced through the bone

I have never abandoned you
My Lord

Although I am a stranger to the World

Although all bids me to go

I will never abandon you my Lord

I am watching, weeping, and waiting my Lord

I am waiting

And All is Good

You

In the heart of the indifference
of the world

I find you

The essence of color

The essence of all essence

And I revive

Slowly

Unfurling like the laugh of a child

Earthly Restaurant

God comes and goes
like a waiter
who never takes my order

I wait patiently at my table
Knowing he's around

Meanwhile I examine the items
in front of me

Plastic flowers
Cheap plates
Dirty table cloth

And I realize

This is going to take a lot longer than I thought

O My God

I found an immense thing
butchered by the sea

It was cold and long and forlorn
and smelled of defeat

I found this thing
The hole of the World

I climbed upon its immensities

Touching tenderly, torched things

I found a suggestion of wings

A celestial larynx

Sinews of gold

Even the afterglow of life

Withering low on the colossal carcass

The Wind struck my face

The cold ocean waves mocked me

It was time to find a new home

Or to sleep, curled forever

Between the marbled lips of a mysterious giant

Waiting for the rebirth of λόγος

The Race of the Bomb

Hiroshima is Man

The savage killing face

Giant carnivorous bees

The butchering Ape

Cooperative Devils

Calculating beasts

They build statues, parks, and palaces

To cover their crimes

But the worm knows

And the gods know

The killing heat

This human furnace

My Lord I Bleed

You have defeated me my Lord
Broken me upon Thy Earthly rack

You have defeated me my Lord
Made me feast upon my Deepest lack

You have defeated me my Lord
Made me see but not touch

You have defeated me my Lord
All things Evil have me in their clutch

You have defeated me my Lord
Made me a poet of the Night

You have defeated me my Lord
Made me curse the water, air, and Light

But in one thing You have not

My wild unruly love for Thee
Bleeds
And will not stop.

Books

Books
Used to be
Precious
Things

Sacred
Cargo

I remember
Tortured men
In tight black
Existential Jackets
And
Heavy accents

Bringing books
To my Grandfather's
Apartment

One of them
Handed me
Les Mots
As if he had
Just revealed
God
To me

I stared
At the old worn book

And smiled

Hard

My poetry
has heavy
balls

Or
At least
I like to think so

I rub it
Hard
My poetry

I make it
Stand
Erect

And since
I'm nuts

I invite you
To suck
On it

To kill

Or

To Fill

You

Or

Both

Last Rites

If I get sick

I'm gonna shoot myself

It's a good way to cut down
On exorbitant hospital bills

If I get sick

I'm gonna send you to hell

Before I blow my skull

But the worse thing is

To know

You were a son of a bitch
In life

And that it is you who will

Give the reading

Of my death

Two Kinds

This kind of love

Can get to hate

Real quick

When I look at you

I just want to slap

You

in the face

To wake you up
In the middle of my hate

To keep you up

In the flames

To remind you

Of the burn
I felt for you

And all those
Stupid looks

On my face

Angry at the Cut

I'm an angry man

No doubt about it

I'm angry at death

Not the final one

Of course

That's natural

But all the man-made ones

The compromises
The lies
The cheats
The double crosses
The masks
The Cunts
The whores
Even
The terminally bored

All those little and bigger
deaths

That make up a Life

The switch-blade

Cuts
Of human existence

Just Like That

Everyone is born with
Nothing to lose

They've already lost

When they first reached
For the tit

Desperate for milk

They already lost

When they first fingered
A wet cunt
Or sucked a hot
Dick

They had deeply lost

When they built a house

Found a job

Published a book

They already lost

But most don't know it yet

Until finally
A crazy mess
Of plastic tubes
Stick out of them
Like a demented porcupine

And they remember
How fast it went

From the tit

To the cunt
To the tube

And wonder
How did it go
Like that

So cheap
So wasted
So soon

Inside Out

The stock market
Plays me

The Traffic lights
Display me

Films
Kaleidoscope me

Books
Speak through me

My very own
Dog
Walks me

My heart
And
My soul
Are the husks
Of structure

And I am all
Inside out

Struggling
With my
Imposed
Invertedness

Go Back!

You fucking
Puritans

Why don't you
Jump
Right
Back in
The Mayflower

And leave
The World
Finally

Alone

Gloriously
Masturbating
Existence

To Rupi Kaur

Two Poets
From
Different Planets

Fucking
each
Other

Making
Alien
Life

Kissing the soup

Screaming difference

Creating something

Blissfully Taboo

What I Believe In

Do I believe in love?

Huh?

I make love

I bring love in

I offer flowers to the Dragon.

I sleep where the moon fears.

I break songs open
like walnuts

Here

Always

Here

New Start

When you're
Divorced

Some people
Believe
(in theory)
That you can
At least
Befriend
A cunt

And that you will
(most likely)
Do so again

That you can wash up
Clean the house
Pay the bills
Look after the kids

At least
That is the hope

But the crazy ones
Know

That for some

Divorce is slipping off
The noose

Finding dead violets
In the snow

Breaking in new horses

Imitating mountains

Watching the sky
For new stars

Alone

Beautifully

Alone

The Eternal Return

Would I wish
To come again?

It is improbable

But nevertheless

Yes

I would stoop and bend and pain
And beg

To once more appear
On the canvas

To be riveted
To light

To play with water

To taste bread

To dance

Dance

Dance

Yes

I would come again

And

Again

Mole

I write poems
Under a million feet
Of dirt

I can't breathe
I can't see
And all I can eat
Is dirt

And more dirt

Yet despite this

I feed my inner disposition

From the moisture
Of the pressure
Of the darkness

And inch by inch

I push up

A blind mole
With hands
Of gold

Drive

I'm just a poet
On a dark road

Waiting for cars
To hit me

Nobody sees me

Because nobody gives
A damn about poetry

I'm mesmerized by
The white and yellow
Lines on the road

They point to the bliss
Of death

I'm going faster now
Down this road

The Wind shaking me

I am speed itself

A poet

At war

With Friction

And all the roads
Of the world

Love and Death

My skull
Cracked open
With love

My guts
Spilled over
Green
With love

My skin
Peeled back
With love

My teeth
Shattered
With love

My hands
Smashed
Themselves
With
Love

My eyes
Incinerated
With
Love

My brain
And
My heart
Pulverized
With love

And in the end

The autopsy simply read:

Love

Dragon

There's a
Dragon
That
Stalks
The
Land

He does not
Reek
(At least not openly)

But he
Seeks
You

On the street
While watching T.V.
While eating dinner

His fumes surround
You

His slow fire
Devours
Your
Essence

You were born
Inside
His dark belly

And you will
Die
Torn and
Disfigured

Under
His watchful
Eternal
Green eyes

Master

There is no God

But there is a Devil

And he made the World

Twist

Around his fingers

Tight

To his heart

The Devil

Laughed

As he saw Men

Build houses of worship

Yet sometimes

He would slip in

Because he liked the music

And the comical sight

Of the hopeful hopeless

The Last Performance

This poisoned clown

Who dies slowly for you

His balloons are all hot

His music box turns

For your lost heart

To bring you the color

That this life cannot

This little dying clown

Smiles a while

Waiting for a sign

That his performance was satisfactory

That the blood on your lips has dried

For a lukewarm clapping

For someone to finally wipe the mascara
From his eyes

Carcass

I am broken in a thousand places

The worms will not eat of me

The vultures will not feast

The falcon passes over

And the lions sleep

Revelation

The Truth did not set me free

It brought me low and the end of love

The Truth did not set me free

But poisoned the breast, the rivers, the pink honey crest

It sought the bright serpent egg

And the hard jaw of death

The Truth did not set me free

But brought me the caretaker's watch

The steel of the bee

The Truth crucifies me

As the sun kneels on my chest

As the night siphons my breath

I silently sob for ignorance

I am illumined

I am tortured

I have crossed the river Jordan

Knowledge thrust upon me like the last earthly kiss

I am one who has been forced to know the mind
Of catastrophic radiance

Worthless

I wrote these poems
On old toilet paper

That's all they're worth

At the end of the world

They won't cure anybody's
Cancer

They won't stop you
Stepping off *that* bridge

They won't help you
Find love

They won't do anything

But sit there

Like shit

In the still waters

Of Existence

Part II
Earlier Poems

I

You who have brought me the Apocalypse
Come dine with me
We will sip cement
And eat the flowery rot
Of your murderous invention
We will tell stories
Of ancient fools
And thirsty seamen
Of the last wail
Of the animal
Of Nature's death
We will dance around
An Electronic table
Displaying Maps
Of Cain and of Abel

Yet we are sleepy now
Deprived of oxygen
As we wait for the final signals
From Mars
To Say: All Flesh is Complete

II

Why is it that I see
The Fire of Man
As a lit cigarette
Dangling
Upon the lips
Of a nervously ambiguous God?

III

I roasted marshmallows
in the Apocalypse.
Why not?
What would you do?

IV

To say I loathe you
Wouldn't do you justice.
I want all your electrons
To flow
Backwards

V

There are worse things than picking up trash
And on the way
You may find love
Standing there
Toothless and Ragged
With burnt palms
Ready for any bright dime

VI

Woe is the honor of the Last Man
To know
To feel
To believe
In a world of ruin
Ruled by steel, wire, and death
To dream the dream of Man
as the last dreamer
To see the doom of All
To be the last failed revolution;

I drown, dying in curses and in love
and you will forget me
as your eyes become accustomed
to worlds ever darker
to Beings of ever greater dread

VII

The maidens of Death come to me
I kiss each one
Soft is their breath
Warm is their terror
I embrace their knowledge
I drink of their Sweet Death
Filling me with the power of oblivion

VIII

To be a fool under a thousand lights
To be the object of power
To be made Distance
To lose all delight and suffer all sorrow
To dream no dream
Shuttered in silence
Laboring under the Sign of Dante and of Sisyphus
The fool screams
The eternal howl of complete darkness

IX

I fell down in my accursed chains
Yet to lift each one
If just a little
Was my Battle Hymn
My Glory beyond Promethean Pain

X

In my arms I held the dead child
longer than creation
until the Voice came and said:
Awake! It is time to place all things
in the River

XI

My eyes were of death
My hands were of death
My tongue spoke of death
My heart ached with death
And yet
I searched every fire

Aleph

XII

Carved strongly by the foreign knife of hate
I bled slowly
all the lessons of blood

XIII

The stars lie down in anguish
to kiss the dark for comfort
once having seen the light
that stirs me to see
to disclose you

XIV

For a love damned from the start
to make stars ash

oceans black
and the full blush of life bleak and bitter
For such love
the shoulders of Atlas are not enough
For like the Gorgon
it cannot gaze upon itself
lest its doomed passions turn to stone
And all the icy heat of this love
choke
And leave the soul a char
tortured and flayed by Night's infinite shore
a plaything revoked
starved and decayed
but held in place
by the impossible accomplishment
by the rhythm and pulse of Satanic joy

XV

In the Human Fields broken and crushed by power
Sunlight seeks absentmindedly its proper place
While the rain seeks in vain
for a Seed
from whence to begin again

XVI

I cry out: "Where is my Lord, God?"
And I am a Voice in the Wilderness
No water can cleanse me
No Sun can warm me
No Wind can soothe me
I am but a Man
A Voice

XVII

Like a deeply angry slumbering sea
cusping the wintry remembrance of oppression
the masses were raised furiously
by cunning water magicians
unafraid of blood spray
and the watery tomb of waves

Part III
Environmental Ethics

Environmental Ethics

I

A Kingly creature; now creatureless King
An Empire out of breath while breathless doing
Air, water, land all three commanded
to remain in place and serve
They wilt under the lash of gentle commerce
whilst jolly plenty stumbles along in filthy blindness
All living things now cringe at the gross summons of Man
Yet meanwhile Gaia gathers up her furious arms in Amazonia,
Under the Sea, and over glacial ridge rallying to expel
this internal invader and push him back either
into oblivious earthly Armageddon
or into the cold mocking stare of the stars

II

The Peculiar Human Gnaw has overtaken all of life
Or was it always to be so?
In more Halcyon days
Every hunger was checked by another
Until Consumption reduced nature's maw
into a tiny red sack of paroxysmal fury
The First Commandment: Feed Naked Ape
Even the Sun must be brought down, ever closer
For the warmth of Gaia only heats up to slowly fade
And towering in power resplendent
is Homo Loquens blithely chattering away his implosive doom

III

All loosen the golden reins of Helios
and arraign the ancient nymphs of the half-hidden alcoves
for all will be measured to new oblivion
and fitted to Faustian forgetfulness
Night shall be cast away under the glare of Argus-Eyed cities

And days shall rush by withered by productive rhythms
And there will be no song, no feast, no true fecundity
For the Lyre is unstrung and rusted
The Banquet tables lain bare
For Today Persephone shall be crowned queen of the underworld forever

IV

For the Mastery of the Word a World was lost
Cold cognition could not coalesce willingly
In nature's corrective undulations
A planet turned into a grey shade of Ape Neo-Cortex
Neurons a-flame; all is fire now
The first flint strike has spread far
The flickering shadows of hungry beasts have been banished by Ape-Fire
The terror of ancient nights has been put to sleep
Yet all encompassing fear has returned in a blinding chariot of luminous flight

V

We eat what we have made
A burning repast of steel, coal, oil, aluminum and innocent flesh and bone
We eat and laugh and laud abundance
in clever circulatory ways
We move the dials of speed and of time
making light of eternity and of vastness
We are larger than the largest
Our grand freedom has enchained the world
We are bad children
who will never escape Mother
Even now her slow smoldering hands reach out
to scorch and to smother our rebellious nonchalance

VI

To sustain the unsustainable beast
To hold a roar that shatters the air
To resist the wave that inundates the shore
To darken the blast that blinds all
This is our unmistakable task
To bind the fateful excellences of Man
Before the remonstrance of the storm

VII

Takanakapsaluk
You have exited the water
leaving trails of yellow-green excrescence
to mark your demise
The watery carcasses of your proud sons and daughters
mock your lugubrious final march
The land has triumphed over water
From whence tiny life emerged
Now broad death gurgles and submerges
Aqueous exile
Choked Goddess
Silent towers of Sand, Salt, and Gypsum will be your curse

VIII

Fire is our true God
In burning we are what we are
The destiny of heat is our story
The flame has shaped our mind and maw
We stare slack jawed and bug eyed into the millennial orange light
Mesmerized by the transmogrifications of energy
We fluorescent shamans
We flash our teeth and powerfully raise our hands
In festivals of fire
We prepare for the coming of cold, ashen nights

IX

The dragons are all here
Every one
St. George seeks his sword in vain
stuck somewhere in a mountain of trash
The banners of our fine crusade
have unfurled throughout the lands
We have been stung by the announcement
of our grand superfluity
We heroes of culture
We villains of the bio-sphere
We are all here
Dragons and knights
Monsters and Madmen
Tangled in hot incomprehensible breath
Grasping one another while slipping down
under the immense spasmodic scales of planetary death

X

Four horrid horses graze knowingly
in the pastures of the Apocalypse
Their Ape-Riders feed them generously
Emerging from electronic shadows of gluttony
the hoots and howling of The Erect Predator
It is a sabbath of Cerebral Gods
Strong sinewy riders of oblivion
Malthus is their half-forgotten stable boy
while The Symphony of Darwin is preparing its final algorithmic coda

XI

The first Gods are nearly dead
They call out their signs in hopes
for the return of The First Shaman
But the New Medicine man deals only
in poisons

He is a careful collector of the dead
Taxidermy has become his reflexive religion
The Chorus of the Gods grows louder
But Mankind like a drunken Oedipus
will continue to defile and to kill
until he will hear the sudden split
and crack
of his blind ontology

XII

Behold: Empire
Do we worship the Big
because we are so small?
We enlarge to desecrate
Vertiginous Profanity!
We will not stop
until we cannot see
An Empire of Native Earth
is not enough
There is talk of stars
of the universe
Was hubris the secret force
that originally set us to walk?

XIII

What can be saved?
The mewing child turns up its face
at a world painted in pain
Threads unspool
Stories are told backwards
We all want to build time-machines
to take us anywhere
but here

Part IV
Medea in Hell

Medea in Hell
(A Short Philosophical One-Act Play)

The Place: Hades (World of Shadows)

Medea:

In that eye within which I saw a world reduced
I engendered a treacly venom so strong
that love itself was sick with weakness and fear
for the sipping of it

Jason:

It was not your love for me that caused you to eternally burn and
to presently kill
but self-love to indignation was firmly tied
with wrath to soothe the scorn you nursed
to arouse the darkest of vipers to curse the living sun

Medea:

You speak too easily of things unknown to you
The fire that first brought forth betrayal
was at first a new foundation of light
For you were the entire spectrum of my existence
beyond father, brother, friend — even our children's life

Jason:

Oh cursed woman! You lie.
It was but simple jealousy that stewed you
to madness and to murder the fruit of your womb
So was your infinite hate incommensurate
to any human love

Hadean Chorus:

To renounce all for love and to lose that love
Is to unloose the soul towards the counsels of hell

Medea:

No good women of Corinth! It was not hell that I sought
but a re-balancing of the world

Hadean Chorus:

But to destroy the innocent in the name of revenge! What terrible logic is this?

Medea:

I am a princess both by nature and by custom and no weak woman
I risked all that I am for the love of *this man* (scowling in Jason's direction)
It was my honor and my rank and my family's love that I set as nothing
before an affection that was more than mortal

Chorus:

And for an affliction that causes the very Gods to cringe in horror!
The blood of thy children! How could a wife's passion murder
the mothering bond! How could you extinguish the very eyes that were the
truest reflection of your own?!?

Medea:

A criminal act was met by another. Simply put: My honor was more terrible
than my motherhood was kind.

Hadean Chorus:

Terrible word: honor. What has not been done in its name. Cities burned. The old, and the weak, and the sick, and the innocent put to the sword. The brave, the good, and the noble vanquished by its unyielding dictate. Honor! You have vanquished all. And no child can beg the smallest reprieve from your impassioned order.

Medea:

Was it not my sacred honor that I gave when I wed this man? Was it not my life's bond that I bore witness to in bearing my brood; in bringing them to life? And when that honor was taken from me did that not drain my life and theirs in an instant of ineffable negation. The unspeakable horror that I felt in annihilating their small bones and trembling hearts was the terrible payment that was due for their illegitimate existence. In falsity conceived, death returned them, myself, and Jason to the Truth.

Hadean Chorus:

If so, then let all Truth be cursed! Let all self, and honor, and revenge be counted amongst the worms. For surely, life it is that we must always follow.

Medea:

You speak of life. I speak of worth. I speak of value. I speak of that which is the very crux of a human life. For we are not worms. For we are not stones. To us is not given the oblivion of mere existence but the unyielding power of saying "Yes" and "No" no matter how terrible the consequence. In going against nature, I re-found myself.

Chorus:

Yes truly spoken unnatural woman! For what emotion, what concept, what idea could figure more highly than a mother's love? You have betrayed the very heart and hearth of all civilization.

Medea:

Is that so? Is it a woman's lot to bathe and to console and to nurture all and everyone that exists around her? Is she mother first and last when entering that celebrated state? Or is there some other existence that she must find that both precedes and follows it? What is on the other side of Woman?

Chorus:

It is surely an adventure with high stakes. Are you strong enough to erect the new Gods that you must find to sustain you upon your eventual arrival to this new sacred place? Will they be strong enough to forgive murder in the name of self-revelation?

Medea:

Oh women of Corinth! I know not. I seek not forgiveness. I do not even seek out any kind of understanding or pity. But I seek. It is a power greater than all the others now. I seek an awakening beyond love and death and murder and betrayal. My deeds are the first acts of rebellion's birth.

Jason:

A bloody revolution yours! To cancel the innocent and the issue of your womb in the name of emancipation! To cover crimes most base with trumped up, glorious names and titles. Thus is every insurgent a criminal and you, like a mad jackal, devour your own kind in the hopes of producing another brood greater and more divine! No crime can be whitewashed with an idea. Every revolution is hate disguised as justice.

Medea:

Oh treacherous husband! Your words betray a world. A world ruled by men blind to the possibility of Woman. Yes, I killed that which was expected of me, defined for me, expressed *as me*. But imagine my surprise when, because of your sovereign acts of perfidy, I realized that all *this was not me*. That in my despair I saw a light that beckoned me to go further, reach deeper, see clearer an horizon that was always there hidden in plain sight. All birth is a painful bargain with death. All beginnings are a farewell. Even murder most malignant can yield new earth.

Jason:

These are the ravings of a madwoman! Mad, bestial, and full of her own proud self. I see nothing here but the deed and the innocent dead.

Medea:

Innocent! Was it innocence when you deceived me about your true intent? Was it innocence when you used my own powers against me? Was it innocence when, for reason of stately advancement, you discarded me? What weapon did you leave me with to revenge my several disgraces if not to maim mine own self? You disfigured my love and so I disfigured yours. The bloody image that I now present to you is the mirror image of your own most horrid teachings. Look upon it. Own it. For I am your newly awakened creature that spits your blackest villainy back at you.

Jason:

And yet, behold your eternal punishment!

(Enter two small disfigured wraith-like children)

Medea:

No! No! My freedom is too great. I cannot look upon it. I dare not look! The sweetest figures of my cruelest damnation for what *I am*, for what I have done. A woman's hate bathed in the blood of a mother's love. A despicable bile gurgling up towards the limits of Men's Rule choking me upon an unseemly feast of fiery justice. Bones. Bones are my loves. A grand wasteland of betrayal and all doubled for my remaining true to my own inner flame. I have done thee greatest wrong my beautiful angels in righting myself. I have swallowed love whole so that I might repudiate the wickedness of men; their unconscionable deeds which neglect desire and extol death. In banishing you to Hades, I restored myself. In thy terrible blood, I damned myself to a fresh world alone, naked, and wretched with my new word "freedom" dangling, mewing savagely upon my lips.

(The wraiths depart)

Jason:

Gorgon! Turn your own deadly eyes upon yourself! For the savageness of your bright new gaze should turn your insides into heaviest stone! Rebellious creature! who charged you to cancel sweet life to pay for slights, insults, and the ancient demeanor of men? What right have you to cancel the buds of innocent Spring? You are no woman but an abomination; damned among the judgements of the Gods and rightfully cursed by the memory of Men.

Medea:

You call me damned. You picture me a fusion of all that is unholy, sick, and unclean. And yet I transcend all your definitions! Within the horror of the deed, sprouts the seed of new beauty, life, and nobility!

Jason:

Nobility?!? What is noble in children's death? What argument can you devise to erase their pleading for their lives in pitiless confrontation with motherly love treacherously perverted into a raging insatiable beast! Cannibal! Monster! Freak! You are the mad flesh that feeds upon itself! You deserve nothing better than to never have been born or to ever have given birth.

Medea:

Yes! Stillborn, that is what you wish me to be. But I live. And will continue. I will bring upon myself all the stark attention of the ages so as to say: "Behold the beautiful monster if you have but the courage to see!". Horror is the thunderous shudder of the speechless agony of new existence. I sacrificed all for those others I could but dimly see in the far distance. From my blood, sorrow, and pain will spring new life and the wicked smile of History will sneer and say: "Es musste so sein!!"

Hadean Chorus:

So this sorrowful tale has no end. In negating Woman; Woman was found. All innocence was betrayed and proper sight restored. The chains of sex were ripped apart and a new womb torn open. Bloody and envious and greedy for life. Medea is both devil and saint depending where you, dear spectator, stand on the continuum of time. Her defiance turns human hearts to half-hidden truths that burn out the rubbish of false consciousness. Her dagger plunges deep again and again into the mystery of subjugation, intimacy, loyalty, and freedom. We are all Medea's children. And we shall live.

124

Part V
Final Kiss

Eternal Kiss

This poem is a kiss
That I wish
To send through time

To hold your lips
To behold your eyes

To never let die
,You,
who I most simply
Love

This poem is a kiss
Most solemn to apply
Again and again
In joy and in pain
In this life and beyond

This poem is a kiss
Which I press upon your lips
For within it is the pulse of life
And eternal ignorance of death

Here, by kissing you,
Time after time
A poem red with life
A poem that prepares the bed
Where we shall sleep
Sharing Kisses like stars
By the mercy of Human remembrance.

ibidem.eu